A portion of the proceeds from every book sold will be donated to
The Food Allergy and Anaphylaxis Network (FAAN) for Food Allergy Research

NO LOBSTER, PLEASE!

A Story of a Child with a Severe Seafood Allergy

*"This delightful story will educate and entertain
children with a seafood allergy.
Their friends will enjoy it too!"*
Anne Muñoz-Furlong, Founder & CEO, The Food Allergy and Anaphylaxis Network

Robyn Rogers
Illustrated by Ms. Fazio's First Grade Class
at the H. Olive Day School

ISBN 0-9726408-0-0

Copyright 2003 by Heartsome Publishing

Library of Congress Control Number: 2002114614

All rights reserved. Published by Heartsome Publishing

Heartsome Publishing
P.O. Box 129
Norfolk, Massachusetts 02056

www.nolobsterplease.com

No part of this publication may be reproduced in whole or part,
or stored in a retrieval system, or transmitted in any form or by any means,
electronic, mechanical, photocopying, recording or otherwise,
without written permission from the publisher.
Printed in Korea By asianprinting.com
Photography by Natural Photos/Margie Soderlund

Design and Pre-press production by Valley Graphics, Foxborough, Massachusetts 02035

This book is dedicated to all of you
who helped make it happen.

I thank you with all my heart.

And, of course, to James,
I hope you continue to live your life without
a care in the world!

Heartsome Publishing

Hi, my name is James.
It is Saturday morning and I just woke up.

I really didn't feel like getting out of bed today.
I am feeling sad.
My family and friends are going to a big lobster party.
I can't go because
lobster makes me very sick.
My mom told me that I am allergic (al-ler-gic) to it.

I found out that I was allergic to lobster when I helped my mom crack her lobster open one night. It made me very sick.

At first I felt so itchy. I got big red bumps and I itched and scratched all over my body! My mom told me that I had hives.

My mouth felt tingly, my tummy hurt, and I felt like I was going to be sick!

When the ambulance got to my house, the paramedics (pa-ra-med-ics) gave me a shot in my leg right away!

They took me to the hospital in the ambulance. My mom got to come with me!

I felt much better after they gave me the shot. They told me I had to go to the hospital and get checked out by the doctor. I didn't mind because they were all so nice to me!

When we were leaving the hospital, the doctors gave my mom some medicine to carry with her all the time, just in case I ever touched lobster again.

She told me that it is called epinephrine (ep-in-ef-rin) or an EpiPen®.

I didn't like the EpiPen® shot, but I knew that it made me all better.

A few days later, my mom took me to a special allergy (al-ler-gy) doctor. I sat on my mom's lap while the nurse took some skin tests on my arm. I didn't cry and it even tickled a little!

When the tests were done, we went into the doctor's office. He told my mom that I wasn't only allergic to lobster, but I was allergic to all shellfish and a lot of other seafood, too. He also told her that I must always stay away from it, and that every time I go near it I could get even sicker than I got before.

You will need this

At first, I felt a little sad and I could tell that my mom did too. My mom made me feel better. She told me that she would make sure that I am always safe. She carried a bag that had my EpiPen® shot in it. Just in case, she took it everywhere I went.

I can't eat out at seafood restaurants or places that have seafood in buffets. In some restaurants, they cook the food in the dining room. If they are cooking seafood, I can't go there either because even the smell can make me sick.

Nurse

At school lunch, I have to sit at a "tuna-free" table, and when they serve fish sticks, I get to eat with the school nurse in her office. The nurse is really nice, and she makes me feel special. It is fun!

Oh, I hear my dad calling my brother and sisters to leave for the lobster party now.

My mom is going to stay home with me. Sometimes I feel badly because lobster used to be my mom's favorite food! She doesn't seem to care about it anymore!

Oh, now I hear my mom calling me. "James, come on, we have a fun day planned! We are going to go to all of your favorite places today!"
See, I knew it wasn't so bad after all!

My mom and I had so much fun today
at all of my favorite places
that I forgot where everyone
else went!

We finished the day at my favorite restaurant. I ordered a grilled cheese sandwich.

My mom told the waitress about my allergy. The waitress told us that she would make sure the cook was very careful with my food so that it doesn't touch any seafood.

After we ate dinner, I wanted to have dessert.
The waitress came over to take our order.
I ordered an ice cream sundae, with a cherry on top!
The waitress wrote it all down and then I said,
"Wait, one more thing,

No lobster, please!"

We all giggled and that was the end of
the best day ever!

Special thanks to
all of my wonderful illustrators,
I couldn't have found better artists anywhere!

Emily Bakinowski,	p. 18	Nathan Johnson,	p. 7
Molly Bartlett,	p. 15	Alexis Lauria,	p. 12
Samuel Bassick,	p. 21	Caroline McBride,	p. 22
Elyse Bechet,	p. 8	Melissa McCarthy,	p. 10
Daniel Boudreau,	p. 11	James Meredith,	p. 23
Jack Boylan,	p. 16	Shea Newman,	p. 9 + 27
Connor Cassidy,	p. 24	Jacob Norris,	p. 17
Melissa Daigle,	p. 14	James Rogers,	p. 5
John Dillon,	p. 20	Kevin Stone,	p. 13
Jeanine Duchaney,	p. 6	Brendan Zimmerman,	p. 25

Ms. Fazio, First Grade Teacher and Cover Designer

Ms. Fazio and Mrs. Conyers, thanks for everything!

Parent Information

Thank you for purchasing "No Lobster, Please!" By making this wise choice, you will not only enjoy the story and learn from it, but you will also help support food allergy research.

Approximately six million Americans have food allergies. A food allergy reaction is caused by your body's immune system overreacting to a protein in the offending food. Peanuts, tree nuts, egg, milk, fish, shellfish, soy, and wheat account for 90% of all food-based allergic reactions. Peanuts, tree nuts, fish, and shellfish are most likely to cause an anaphylactic (life threatening) reaction. Many children will outgrow an allergy to milk, soy, wheat, and eggs. Peanuts, tree nuts, fish, and shellfish tend to be life-long allergies.

Food allergy symptoms can range from mild to life threatening and usually occur within minutes of ingesting, touching, or inhaling the offending protein. The symptoms may include any or all of the following: hives; vomiting; diarrhea; cramping; swelling of the throat, lips or tongue; difficulty breathing or swallowing; a metallic taste or itching of the mouth; generalized flushing; itching or redness of the skin; nausea; increased heart rate; plunging blood pressure; sudden feeling of weakness, anxiety, or an overwhelming sense of doom; collapse; or loss of consciousness.

Food allergies need to be taken seriously and everyone needs to be aware of the symptoms, as they can occur at any age and any time. Being aware can save a child's life.

"Education is the key to managing allergies in a school setting. "No Lobster, Please!" is an effective and enjoyable vehicle for conveying important, possibly life-saving, information to the peers of children with food allergies. James's first-hand account of his seafood allergy conveys information that is meaningful and entertaining to our young students and builds a foundation for understanding and sensitivity. Our school gives it 1,200 "Thumbs Up"!
   Linda A. Balfour, Principal, H. Olive Day School

"Robyn Rogers has created a book which relates to all age groups from child to adult. It is a story that is not often told but is now available for all to read. It is a perspective of what modifications a young boy and his family must make to their lives together. This story goes beyond one family into the homes of many families. I strongly recommend it for all to read."
   Leo Fantini, Principal, Freeman Centennial School

"This book is an excellent learning tool for friends and classmates of children with a seafood allergy."
   Ann Hurley, R.N., School Nurse, H. Olive Day School

"No Lobster, Please! is a marvelous resource to teach children how to accept and understand the realities of seafood allergies."
   Lori Fazio, First Grade Teacher, H. Olive Day School

"This book is a valuable resource for parents and teachers. It creates a heightened awareness of a child's severe allergic reaction to seafood. Robyn Rogers has written the story in a narrative easy-to-read format from her child's personal experiences. Parents and young children will gain a better understanding of this health concern. I commend Robyn for bringing this information to the forefront."
   Janet M. Bloom, M.Ed., First Grade Teacher, H. Olive Day School

"Children often have difficulty understanding and coping with the medical problems of others. Is it catchy? Why does he (she) have to do XYZ? What will happen to him? How did she get it? In "No Lobster, Please!" Robyn Rogers cleverly explains to children in story format exactly what it means to have a serious food allergy. Her straightforward presentation of this condition, from the afflicted child's perspective is calm, informational, and demystifying. Thank you, Robyn, for drawing upon your own experience with James to provide an important learning experience to children, their parents, and their teachers as well."
   Simone Favaloro, Second Grade Teacher, H. Olive Day School